AF522330

Water Quality Analysis

NIPA® GENX ELECTRONIC RESOURCES & SOLUTIONS P. LTD.
New Delhi-110 034

About the Authors

Dr. Shivendra Kumar is Professor & Head, Department of Aquaculture, College of Fisheries, Dr. Rajendra Prasad Central Agricultural University, Pusa, Bihar, with over 16 years of experience in teaching, research, and extension. He holds M.F.Sc. and Ph.D. in Fish Nutrition and Biochemistry from ICAR-CIFE, Mumbai. Dr. Kumar has made significant contributions to sustainable aquaculture through the development of low-cost fish feed, nutritional programming, and eco-friendly technologies like Litchi Waste-Based Fish Feed, Pond Polyhouse for prawn culture, and a patented Solar-Powered Fish Preservation and Transportation Cart. He has led in over 17 national and international research projects. Dr. Kumar has authored more than 70 research papers (2300+ citations, h-index 23, i10-index 34), 6 books, 35 book chapters, policy briefs, and numerous scientific articles. His work on molecular biomarkers, micronutrient delivery systems, and fish meal replacements has advanced fish nutrition and health. He is the recipient of several honors, including the Dr. N. R. Menon Best Postgraduate Thesis Award, Dr. Hiralal Choudhury Young Scientist Award, and a post-doctoral fellowship at HAKI, Hungary. In recognition of his contributions to fisheries science, recently he has been awarded as a Fellow of the Bihar Agricultural Science Academy (BASA).

Dr. Rajive Kumar Brahmchari is an Assistant Professor (Sr. Scale) at the College of Fisheries, Dr. Rajendra Prasad Central Agricultural University, Dholi, Bihar. He specializes in Aquatic Animal Health Management, with research interests in parasitology, nanoparticle-based parasite control, and the development of prophylactic strategies to prevent disease outbreaks in aquaculture. His academic and research focus includes fish health management, immunology, and toxicology of commercially important fish species. Dr. Brahmchari has authored several research articles in national and international peer-reviewed journals, as well as book chapters, practical manuals, and outreach materials aimed at advancing health management practices in aquaculture systems. Presently, he is handling the PMMSY-funded NSPAAD Phase II project as Principal Investigator, which focuses on enhancing aquatic animal disease surveillance and diagnostics across the Bihar.

Dr. Sujit Kumar Nayak holds Ph.D. in Fish Pathology and Microbiology from the Central Institute of Fisheries Education, Mumbai. Currently, he is working as an Assistant Professor-cum-Scientist at the College of Fisheries, Dholi (Dr. Rajendra Prasad Central Agricultural University, Bihar). His research focuses on Aquatic Animal Health Management. Dr. Nayak has received notable recognitions, including the Emerging Scientist Award (2020) and Young Scientist Award in Fisheries Science (2022). Dr. Nayak has guided several M.F.Sc students and published 34 research papers in reputed national and international peer-reviewed journals. Additionally, he serves as a reviewer for various scientific journals, supporting the advancement of research in fisheries science. Through his dedicated work in teaching, research, and extension activities, Dr. Nayak continues to make significant contributions to the field of fisheries and aquaculture in India.

Dr Archana Sinha is working as Head and Principal Scientist in Aquatic Environmental Division Biotechnology Division of ICAR-CIFRI, Barrackpore, Kolkata has served the nation for 35 years in the field of fisheries research, education and extension. Completed successfully about 50 research projects including external funded. Contributed immensely in fisheries education by teaching Ph.D.; M. F. Sc.; Diploma in Fisheries Management and Administration; Certificate course in Inland fisheries Administration etc. for 20 years. Guided 10 nos. Ph.D. students for their thesis and 30 nos. of students for their dissertations. Organized more than 100 need based Short Term Training Programme (STP) for fish farmers, students, women and educated youth. Published about 200 research papers in International and National journals, 8 books, 50 book chapters, more than 50 Training manual and a number of popular articles in English and Hindi including extension leaflets. Received several awards and Fellowship of ICAR, Ministry of Science and Technology and different Professional Societies.

Dr. Prem Prakash Srivastava did his graduation, and post-graduation from University of Allahabad in Biochemistry and Doctorate from VBS University, Jaunpur and is a known academician in Fisheries, and now Dean, College of Fisheries, Dholi, Muzaffarpur Bihar under Dr. Rajendra Prasad Central Agricultural University, Pusa, Bihar. He began his career at ICAR-CIFE, Mumbai, and held key positions at ICAR-NBFGR and ICAR-CIFE, including Principal Scientist, Controller of Examinations, and Dean, Student Welfare. He also served as the first Registrar of RPCAU. He is now

Dean, College of Fisheries, Dholi, Muzaffarpur Bihar under Dr. Rajendra Prasad Central Agricultural University (RPCAU), Pusa, Bihar. Dr. Srivastava has more than 35 years of experience in the field of Fisheries Research and Teaching where he has successfully planned and executed several projects for ensuring quality research in Fish Nutrition, Fish Biochemistry, Fish Physiology, Nutrigenomics areas. Dr. Srivastava has guided over 90 M.F.Sc. and Ph.D. students and published 250+ papers. His research focuses on fish nutrition, biochemistry, physiology, and nutrigenomics. He has received numerous awards, including the Dr. Zahoor Qasim Gold Medal, Dr. Belsare Gold Medal, and Fellowships from FASET and Bioved Research Society, recognizing his outstanding contributions to fisheries science and education.

Water Quality Analysis

A Laboratory Manual for Aquaculture Practices

Authors

Shivendra Kumar
R.K. Brahmchari
Sujit Kumar Nayak
Archanan Sinha
Prem Prakash Srivastava

Technical Assistance

Diwakar Prakash
Maneesh Kumar Dubey
Rinki Kumari

NIPA® GENX ELECTRONIC RESOURCES & SOLUTIONS P. LTD.
New Delhi-110 034

Technical Assistance:

The Authors and Publisher are Thankful to: Diwakar Prakash, Maneesh Kumar Dubey and Rinki Kumari

NIPA® GENX ELECTRONIC RESOURCES & SOLUTIONS P. LTD.

101,103, Vikas Surya Plaza, CU Block
L.S.C. Market, Pitam Pura, New Delhi-110 034
Ph : +91-11-43860225, Mob.: +91 9717133558, 9540816132
E-mail: newindiapublishingagency@gmail.com
Website: www.nipaersources.com

Print ISBN: 978-93-72198-13-3

ebook ISBN: 978-93-72190-83-0

Composed and Designed by NIPA®.

Dr Atul K Singh
Vigyan Ratna (Govt. of UP)
Former Director ICAR-CICFR &
Emeritus Scientist ICAR-NBFGR

Foreword

Water is the cornerstone of aquaculture—its quality directly affects the health, growth, and productivity of aquatic life. As aquaculture rapidly evolves to meet the growing global demand for sustainable food, maintaining optimal water conditions has become more essential than ever.

It is with great pleasure that I write the foreword for ***Water Quality Analysis: A Laboratory Manual for Aquaculture Practices***. This timely manual arrives at a critical moment in the aquaculture sector's growth, as the industry increasingly emerges as a pillar of global food security. Amidst all the advancements and innovations, one fundamental truth endures: water quality remains the foundation of sustainable and successful aquaculture operations.

This manual is designed to be a practical and reliable guide for students, researchers, technicians, and professionals in aquaculture and aquatic sciences. It offers clear, step-by-step instructions for analyzing crucial water quality parameters—including dissolved oxygen, pH, ammonia, nitrite, nitrate, hardness, and alkalinity—that shape the dynamics of aquaculture systems.

What sets this manual apart is its balance of clarity, usability, and scientific precision. It simplifies complex analytical techniques into accessible protocols that are easily implemented in both laboratory and field environments. More than a procedural guide, it cultivates a deep understanding of water chemistry and equips users to interpret results critically and make informed, impactful decisions.

I commend the authors for their diligent work in producing a resource that is both scientifically robust and user-friendly. Their thoughtful integration of practical application with academic rigor reflects a strong grasp of the evolving needs of the aquaculture community. I am confident that this manual will serve not only as an essential laboratory tool but also as a stepping stone in nurturing a generation of aquaculture professionals who are both technically skilled and environmentally responsible.

This manual will no doubt find a lasting place in academic curricula, commercial hatcheries, research labs, and farms—wherever water quality is recognized as the key to aquaculture success.

July 16, 2025

(A.K.Singh)

Preface

Fish farming can be a profitable source of income, provided that farmers diligently manage all aspects of the operation. Fundamental to this management is maintaining high water quality, which is crucial for the health and growth of fish and other aquatic organisms. Poor water quality can hinder growth and even lead to mortality, making water quality analysis a key factor in the success of aquaculture. Water quality parameters are categorized into physical, chemical, and biological factors. Among these, certain parameters such as temperature, dissolved oxygen, pH, salinity, ammonia, nitrate, and nitrite are particularly important due to their tendency to fluctuate significantly. Even slight changes in these parameters can stress cultured organisms or negatively impact their health. Therefore, regular monitoring of these water quality parameters is essential to ensure optimal production of fish and other aquatic species.

Fish are cold-blooded and rely on the surrounding water temperature to regulate their body temperature. Water temperature is the most critical physical factor affecting the survival and growth of fish, influencing their activity levels, behaviour, feeding, growth, and reproduction. Each species has its own tolerance and optimal temperature range. When water temperatures fall outside this optimal range, a fish's body temperature may become too high or too low, adversely affecting growth and potentially leading to death. The pH level of pond water can range from acidic to alkaline and unfavourable pH levels can be harmful to fish. Most fish cannot survive for extended periods in water with a pH below 4 or above 11. The optimal pH range for most fish species is between 6.5 and 8.5. Additionally, insufficient dissolved oxygen in pond water can lead to poor feeding behaviour, with fish often refusing food and frequently swimming near the water's surface in search of oxygen. In summary, successful fish farming hinges on meticulous management of water quality. Regular monitoring and maintenance of key physical and chemical parameters are essential to ensure the health, growth, and productivity of cultured fish and other aquatic organisms.

It is crucial for new farmers and entrepreneurs in aquaculture to understand water quality parameters and their impact on cultured animals to maximize fish production while minimizing input costs. By receiving proper training and staying updated on water quality management techniques, they can ensure optimal conditions in their ponds. Aquaculture entrepreneurs should be familiar with the basics of water quality management, including how to properly collect and analyse water samples. This manual serves as a comprehensive guide, covering twenty-one essential water parameters along with detailed materials and methods. By following the guidelines in this manual, farmers can effectively manage the water quality in their aquatic environments, leading to healthier and more productive fish populations.

Authors

Contents

Contents

Abbreviations

lit	:	Liter
mL	:	Milliliter
mg	:	Milligram
°C	:	Degree Celsius
Wi	:	Initial weight
Wf	:	Final weight
ppt	:	Parts per thousand
PSU	:	Practical salinity units
NTU	:	Nephelometric Turbidity unit
DO	:	Dissolved oxygen
BOD	:	Biochemical oxygen demand
COD	:	Chemical oxygen demand
DOi	:	Initial dissolve oxygen
DOf	:	Final dissolved oxygen
D.F.	:	Dilution factor
CO_2	:	Carbon dioxide
N	:	Normality
M	:	Molarity
EBT	:	Eriochrome Black T
EDTA	:	Ethylenediamine tetraacetic acid
HCl	:	Hydro chloric acid
TPC	:	Total plate count
CFU	:	Colony forming units

1

Introduction

Aquaculture is practiced in the majority of countries worldwide, however the significance of water quality standards remains largely unknown to farmers and new aqua entrepreneurs. They may achieve maximum fish production with minimal input costs if they are trained and stay up to date on water quality management in the aquatic ecosystem. The water quality categorised into three main of metrics as physical, chemical, and biological parameters. Dissolved oxygen (DO), biochemical oxygen demand (BOD), free carbon dioxide (CO_2), pH, temperature, total dissolved solids (TDS), turbidity, ammonia, nitrite, nitrate, alkalinity, bacterial density primary productivity (chl *a*), plankton population, etc. play a significant role for fish production. However, even small variations in certain physical and chemical parameters—particularly pH, temperature, and dissolved oxygen (DO)—can cause stress in the animals, which may manifest as physiological changes, reduced reproductive capability, and altered behavior. Water parameters such as alkalinity and hardness are relatively stable, whereas others like pH, dissolved oxygen (DO), and temperature fluctuate regularly. Proper maintenance and monitoring of these water quality parameters in aquatic environments support fish health and enhance fish production. On the other hand, variability in dissolved ammonia, nitrites, and nutrients like nitrate significantly affects aquaculture production. It has also been observed that high feeding rates in aquafarms create eutrophic conditions in water bodies, leading to substantial algal blooms. These blooms are responsible for die-offs, and as a result, ammonia levels in the ponds rise rapidly. The environmental factors responsible for generating high ammoniacal concentrations may also lead to increased nitrite concentration in aquafarm. Both ammonia and nitrite are directly toxic or sublethal cultured aqua animals, leading to reduced resistance to diseases. In aquaculture system, ammonia is produced through the ammonification process, which occurs when organic matter is broken down by the microbial community. However, this decomposition also reduces dissolved oxygen levels in the system. Low dissolved oxygen surges the toxicity of ammonia to cultured animals. Ionized ammonia (NH_4^+) and hydroxide ions occurs in equilibrium with unionized aqueous ammonia solution. The unionized form of ammonia (NH_3) is toxic due to its high lipid solubility, which allows it to diffuse readily across cell membranes. Ammonia is utilized as an energy source by nitrifying bacteria such as Nitrosomonas and Nitrobacter, which convert it to nitrite and then nitrate through oxidation. In aquaculture, the primary source of nutrients is feed. When large amounts of feed are added to ponds, the excess feed, fecal matter, and other metabolic byproducts become available in significant quantities, promoting the growth of algae and microorganisms. Maintaining good water quality is essential for the survival and optimal growth of cultured organisms. Therefore, it is important to establish a standardized water quality testing protocol suited to specific conditions.

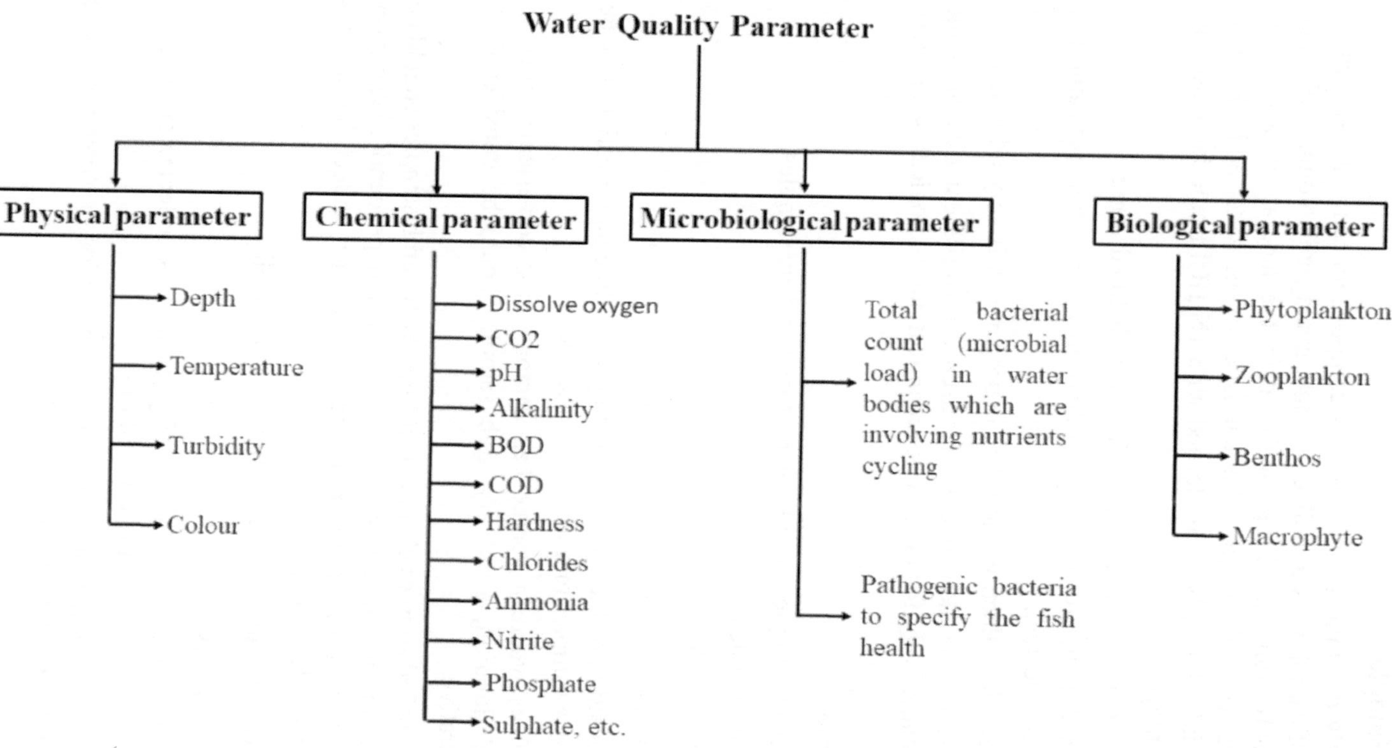

Water Quality Parameter
Physical parameter
Depth
Temperature
Turbidity
Colour
Chemical parameter
Dissolve oxygen
CO2
pH
Alkalinity
BOD
COD
Hardness
Chlorides
Ammonia
Nitrite
Phosphate
Sulphate, etc.
Microbiological parameter
Total bacterial count (microbial load) in water bodies which are involving nutrients cycling
Pathogenic bacteria to specify the fish health
Biological parameter
Phytoplankton
Zooplankton
Benthos
Macrophyte

Collection of Samples

Water is a highly dynamic system, and its components can vary over time. The objective of sampling is to collect a small, manageable volume of water that can be easily transported and analyzed in the laboratory, while still being representative of the overall characteristics of the water body. Prior to sampling, the vials should be acid-cleaned with 1N HCl in the laboratory to ensure sample integrity.

- Sample bottles should be rinsed with clean/distilled water
- Samples should be collected separately from a place where the sampling bottles were cleaned.
- Proper Sample collection should be in proper way is very important
- Samples should be taken in replicates to ensure a representative sampling of the aquatic body for the physicochemical and biological parameters analysis.

Types of samples

1. Grab or catch samples, also known as spot or snap samples.
2. Composite samples.
3. Integrated samples.

1. Grab or catch samples

Only the composition of the source at that specific time and location may be characterised by a samples that were collected there.

- In instances where a source has demonstrated consistency over an extended duration, a solitary grab sample should be considered as demonstrative.
- If the identified sources change over time are to, grab samples should be collected at proper time intervals and analyse independently. Whenever the source composition differs in spatial scale then collect the samples from applicable locations.
- The analysis results may be recognized statistically.

2. Composite samples

Composite samples are a combination of grab samples collected at the same sampling point/site at different interval of times.

- A composite sample represent a shorter time period or a complete cycle of a period operation may be preferable.

- Collect minimum 120-150mL of water sample in every hr, or even 30 minutes at in certain cases (if composition changes every hour). Mix the sample in one bottle after end of sampling period.
- Final volume should be between 4 to 5 lit.

3. Integrated samples

The best way to offer the information required for a given purpose is to analyse a combination of grab samples that were concurrently taken from several sites. These types of samples are helpful for rivers or streams whose composition varies in both width and depth. A specialized sampling instrument is required for the collection of integrated samples.

- The Sample is taken without disturbing the surface water at a predetermined depth.

Preservation of samples

Parameters	Preservation method	Maximum holding period
Colour	Store at 4°C	24 h
Turbidity	Store at 4°C	48 h
DO	Instant analyse on site	6h
BOD	Store at 4°C	6h
COD	2 mL H_2SO_4/L	7 day
Alkalinity	Store at 4°C	24 h
Ammonia	Add 2 mL 40% H_2SO_4 to pH< 2, store at low temperature, analyse as soon as possible	24 h
Nitrate	Analyse as soon as possible	-
Phosphorous	40 mg HgCI/L, store at 4°C.	24 h
Sulphate	Store at 4 °C	7 days
Bacterial Plate count	store samples at 4 °C	36 h

Emerging Water Sampling Technology

In the constantly developing domain of environmental monitoring, new technologies are redefining water sampling methods, making it easier and more effective to assess aquatic ecosystems. Traditionally, water sampling from lakes, ponds, reservoirs and other water bodies used to be a time-consuming process involving much manpower and logistical organization. However, with innovations in drone systems, autonomous surface vehicles (ASVs), IoT devices, and artificial intelligent tools, automated sampling is emerging as a key method for measuring water quality. Here's an insight into the most critical water sampling methods of the current age.

1. Drone-Based Water Samplers

Drones equipped with water sampling payloads which are transforming the way to collect samples in environment. These flying robots can access difficult or dangerous areas, such as ponds with steep banks or shallow zones with limited access, large reservoirs, lakes etc. without putting personnel at risk. By flying to a specific GPS location, drones lower a tube or container into the water to collect a sample and then return to the base station. The AgEagle's drone samplers and modified hexacopter drones with servo-activated grabbers or vacuum samplers offer flexibility, speed, and the ability to consistently sample at specific depths.

Advantages

- **Access to challenging locations:** Drones can reach remote or hazardous areas.
- **Consistent depth sampling:** Drones can collect samples from specific water layers.
- **Efficiency:** Quick sampling across large bodies of water, reducing the time required for data collection.

2. Autonomous Surface Vehicles (ASVs)

Autonomous Surface Vehicles (ASVs) are small robotic boat-like devices that advance autonomously along the water surface for sample gathering. ASVs can run indefinitely without the need for human intervention, sampling water at regular intervals or depths based on onboard sensors and GPS directions. Examples of such include the Platypus (Clearpath Robotics) and Ecomapper AUV, not only for sample water gathering but for creating a map of water depth as well as water quality parameter measurements.

Advantages

- **Continuous, autonomous operation:** No manual input required, ideal for long-term monitoring.
- **Comprehensive data collection:** Equipped with multi-parameter probes (pH, turbidity, DO) and GPS.
- **Versatility:** Can map bathymetry and provide real-time water quality assessments.

3. IoT-Based Fixed Water Samplers

Fixed samplers with IoT enable continuous, real-time sampling from targeted locations within a water bodies. These units, usually floating on the surface of the water, have multi-parametric sensors that measure from temperature to turbidity. The YSI EXO2 Multiparameter Sondes as well as the Aqua TROLL 500 are top systems within the category. These units make it possible for sample collection to trigger automatically based on time settings or sensor reading thresholds, for example, on an ammonia spike.

Advantages

- **Real-time monitoring:** Immediate access to water quality data from stationary platforms.
- **Automated triggers:** Can collect samples based on specific conditions or scheduled times.
- **Cloud connectivity:** Data can be remotely accessed and analyzed for fast decision-making.

4. AI-Controlled Smart Samplers

Artificial intelligence is helping make water sampling smarter through the utilization of sensor information and past patterns for deciding the best times and places for sampling. AI systems are able to anticipate where and when samples need to be taken following a strong storm, for instance, during sunrise, or after a temperature discrepancy through massive databases of past water quality and climatic information. For instance, an AI system can identify a temperature discrepancy within a pond and instruct a drone or ASV to grab a sample from the exact area.

Advantages

- **Intelligent decision-making:** Optimizes the timing and location of sample collection.
- **Predictive capabilities:** AI helps foresee potential pollution events or water quality changes.
- **Efficient use of resources:** Reduces unnecessary sampling and focuses efforts on critical times or areas.

Monitoring Critical Water Parameters: Devices for Precision

The wide array of water parameters ranging from pH and dissolved oxygen (DO) through ammonia, turbidity, and pathogens can be continually measured using sophisticated sensors. Devices like the YSI EXO2 Sonde and the Aqua TROLL 500 can measure several water quality indicators simultaneously. These sensors are part of water sampling instrumentation, providing environmental scientists with accurate, timely information on everything from concentrations of nutrients to algae blooms.

Key water quality parameters and their corresponding devices include:

- **pH, DO, and temperature:** Measured by YSI EXO2 Sonde, Aqua TROLL 500, and DJI Matrice 300.
- **Nutrients and ammonia:** Detected by YSI EXO2 Sonde, Z-Boat 1800RP, and Ecomapper AUV.
- **Chlorophyll-a and TSS:** Monitored by NEMO by Nido Robotics, DJI Matrice 300, and Ecomapper AUV.
- **Pathogens (e.g., E. Coli):** Identified via eDNA Sampling Systems and PONAR DNA Sampler.

Figure (a): Water sampling through Drone

Figure (b): Water sampling through Rope subway

Figure (c): Collection of plankton

Figure (d): Collection of soil sediment

2

Colour

Water colour is consequences of the plankton, humus, metal ions (iron and manganese), weeds and peat materials, presence in water. Iron oxides cause reddish color whereas Manganese oxides causes brown or brackish colour in water. Water colour of an aquatic body also indicates the density of planktons. Brownish colouration without any foul smell is an indication of good growth of zooplankton. Phytoplankton or algae are usually green in colour and these green alage in large quantities turn the green color of water. Water color suggests plankton or other aquatic life growth, clear and transparent colour of water indicates low and poor growth of plankton. Brownish green to greenish brown colour of water indicates well for aquaculture.

Principle

Natural waters colour comprising yellow-brownish in appearance. It has been observed that potassium chloroplatinate (K_2PtCl_2) tinted with small amounts of $CoCl_2$ yield colours that are very much like the natural colours of water. 1 mg/L of Pt (K_2PtCl_6) produces a standard 1 unit of colour. The intensity of colour increases as pH rises. For this reason recording pH together with colour is advisable.

1mg/L Pt (K_2PtCl_6) = 1true colour unit (TCU) =1 Hazen unit (Hz)

Apparatus and glassware

1. pH meter
2. Spectrophotometer
3. Nessler tube
4. Funnel
5. Pipettes
6. Filter Paper (Whatman No. 41)

Reagents

1. **Stock standard colour solution:** 0.5 g crystallized $CoCl_2$. H_2O and 0.823g K_2PtCl_6 dissolve in Deionized water then filter it to remove any

minor turbidity. Add 50 mL conc. HCl and dilute with deionized water to500 mL. The prepared solution has 500 Hazen unit of colour.

2. **Working standard colour solution:** Take 50 ml nessler tubes and prepare different Hazen units. For preparation of 5,10,15,20,25,30,35,40,45,50,60 and 70 Hazen units add 0.5, 1.0, 1.5, 2.0, 2.5, 3.0, 3.5, 4.0, 4.5, 5.0, 6.0 and 7mL of stock coloured solution in 50mLNessler's tube and filled with distilled water up to the mark. These prepared working standards may work for several months but these solutions should be protected from dust and evaporation.

Procedure

1. To get rid of the turbidity, filter the sample through a glass fibre filter paper (0.45μm).
2. Using a spectrophotometer set to measure wavelengths between 385 and 470 nm, find the optical density (OD). Assemble the reference cell with filtered water.
3. Draw a calibration graph (range 10 to 70 units).
4. Record as colour to the nearest whole number.

Calculation

$$\text{Normality of thiosulffate} = \frac{X \times 50}{Y}$$

Where,

X = Estimated colour of a diluted sample

Y = mL of sample taken for dilution

50 = Total volume of sample in Nessler's tube

Colour interpretation

- 0-5 TCU- colourless, less productivity
- 5-50 TCU- slightly coloured, brownish green to greenish brown, phytoplankton and zooplankton productivity.
- >50 TCU- indicates pollution, algal blooms and humic content.
- >100 TCU- strong coloration and undesirable for drinking and aquaculture.

3

pH

pH is defined as the negative logarithm of hydrogen ion concentration. The amount of the acidic gas CO_2 significantly affects the pH of natural water body. Fish have usually blood pH levels of 7.4, but little deviation has been observed, perhaps 7.0 to 8.5pH range is more suitable for the growth and reproduction of the fish. However, pH range 4.0 to 6.5 and 9.0 to 11.0 cause fish death in water pH less than 4.0known as acidic death point or even more than 11.0 known as alkaline death point. The pH of fresh water more fluctuating as compare to sea water due to release and consumption of CO_2 and O_2 respectively by bacterial oxidation and respiration. However, the pH of marine water often constant at 7.8-8.3 due to presence of buffer like $HCO3^-$, CO_2^-, $CO3^{-2}$ etc.

$$ph = \log_{10} \frac{1}{\left[H^+\right]}$$

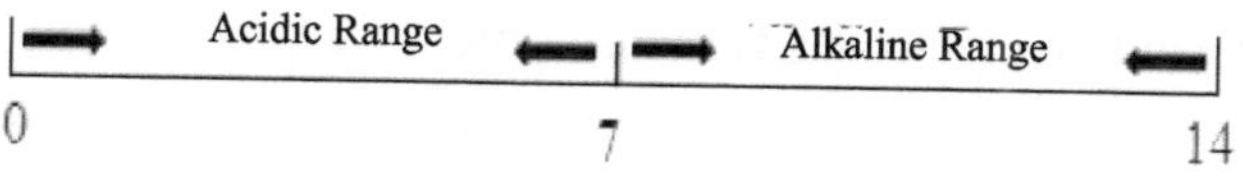

Acidic Range | Alkaline Range

0 — 7 — 14

pH Scale

Principle

The estimation of hydrogen (H^+) ion activity through sensing electrode. Electrode composed of a narrow glass bulb with fixed concentration of HCI solution inside it. A wire made of an Ag-AgCI placed in to the bulb which work as electrode to fix voltage. Potential difference forms between the solution in the glass bulb and the sample solution when the electrode immersed into solution.

The Nernst equation is used to formulate the potential difference E.

$$E = \frac{RT}{nF} \log \frac{K}{Mn+}$$

Where,

E = Half-cell potential

R = Gas constant

T = Temperature

n = Valence

F = Faraday constant

K = Constant

M = ions to be measured

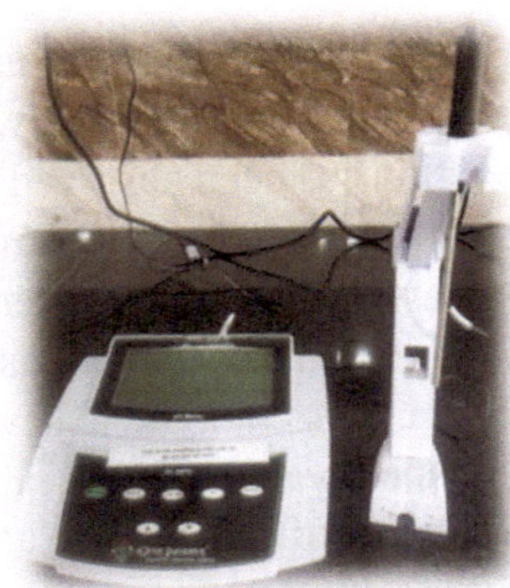

Fig. Digital pH meter

The E (half-cell potential) cannot be measured alone. If the glass electrode is placed against a reference electrode (usually the calomel electrode), the potential difference between two electrodes is measurable. (E - Ecal).

Reagents

Standard buffer tablets (pH 4,7and 9.2) are commercially available. Buffer of different pH can be prepared by dissolving standard pH tablets in distilled water. The above buffer solution can be prepared as follows:

1. **Phthalate buffer (pH 4.0 at 25°C):** Dissolve 5.06 g of potassium hydrogen phthalate (KHC_8HP_4) in distilled water to make 500 ml of buffer.
2. **Phosphate buffer (pH 7.0 at 25°C):** Dissolve 1.7 g of KH_2PO_4 & 2.225 g of $Na_2\ HPO_4.2H_2O$ in distilled water to make 500ml of buffer.
3. **Borax buffer (pH 9.18 at 25°C):** Dissolve 1.905g of sodium tetraboratedecahydrate ($Na_2B_4O_7.10H_2O$) in distilled water to make 500 ml of buffer.

Methods to calibrate pH meter

1. Read the operating instructions of pH meter's before using it.
2. Calibrate the pH metre using standard buffer solutions (pH 4.01, 7.0 and 10.01)

3. Clean the electrode by distilled water and dip it in a buffer at pH then slowly adjust the temperature knob to the desired ambient/room temperature.
4. Then again repeat the above procedure with pH 4.01 and 10.01 buffer and adjust meter accordingly.

Sample analysis

1. After calibration, rinse the probe with distilled water, dry with a soft tissue paper, place in sample solution.
2. In order to ensure homogeneity and minimise CO_2 trapping, agitate the sample slightly to establish equilibrium between electrodes and sample.
3. Keep the electrode dipped in storage solution when not in use.

4

Transparency (Secchi Disc Method)

The Secchi disc is named after its Italian inventor Pietro Angelo Secchi. Transparency is a water-quality characteristic of lakes and reservoirs and can be measured quickly and easily using simple equipment. This characteristic varies with the combined effects of colour and turbidity. Some variation may also occur with light intensity and with the apparatus used.

Procedure

1. Morning (early) or afternoon (late) is suitable time to check transparency
2. Lower the Secchi disc and observed the depth at which it just disappears from view (L_1)
3. Then further lift up slowly till it just reappears (L_2).

Calculate as follows

$$\text{Transparency (Secchi disc)} \frac{L_1 + L_2}{2}$$

- For example, if disappearing value (L_1) = 30cm and reappearing value (L_2) is 25 cm

  Then transparency = Transparency (Secchi disc) = (L_1 +L_2)/2

  = (30+25)/2 =55/2 = 27.5 cm.

  Transparency = 27.5cm
- Safe range for carp aquaculture the transparency should be 25-30 cm.

Fig. Secchi Disc

5

Total Solids

Principle

The estimation of all solids, including dissolved, volatile, and suspended solids, is called total solids (TS). The residue that remains after the unfiltered sample evaporates between 103 and 105°C can be used to estimate total solids. Total dissolved solids (TDS) and Total suspended solids (TSS) are its two constituent components. After heating to 550°C, each fraction is separated once more into fixed solids and volatile suspended solids (VSS). The percentage of ash that remains is called fixed solids, while VSS is the organic proportion that was lost as CO_2.

Apparatus

1. Ceramic or platinum evaporating dishes 100 mL volume.
2. Dessicator contain $CuSO_4.5H_2O$. Desiccator, provided with a desiccant containing a colour indicator of moisture ($CuSO_4.5H_2O$).
3. Analytical balance
4. Hot air oven

Procedure

1. Take a clean evaporating beaker or dish of required volume and dry it at hot air oven at 103 to 105°C for 1h, then cool and store it in a desiccator until needed. Immediately weigh before use.

   Note » the initial weight (Wi) in mg.
2. Take 250-300 ml or required volume of unfiltered well mixed sample in it (beaker or dish).
3. Place it in hot air oven at 103 to 105 °C for 2 h.
4. Cool it in a desiccator and take the final weight (Wf) in mg.
5. Replication the above process until a constant weight is achieved

Calculation

$$\text{Total solids (mg / L)} = \frac{(\text{Wf - Wi}) \times 1000}{\text{Volume of sample, ml}}$$

Where Wf = final weight of sample

Wi = initial weight of sample

For example if the sample volume is 100 ml, initial weight of sample 80 and final sample weight after evaporation is 50 then- (80-50) x 1000/100 = 300 mg/l So the estimated total solid will be 300 mg/l

- The ideal range of tatal solid for fish culture should be less than 500 mg/l.

6

Electrical Conductivity

Pure water is a poor conductor of electricity. Water may carry electricity fairly well when it contains electrolytes such as Acids, bases and salts. Electrolytes in the solution dissociates with cations and anions and pass on electrical conductivity. Hence, more electrolytes concentration in water, more its electrical conductance. The following ions are crucial for adding conductivity to water.

i) Cations: Mg^{2+},Ca^{2+}, Na^+ and K^+

ii) Anions: Cl^-, S_4^-, CO_3^-, $HCO_3^-$and NO_3^-

In the International System of units (SI) the reciprocal of ohm is the Siemens (S) and conductivity is reported as millisiemens per meter (mS/m).

1 mS/m = 10 μS/cm = 10 μmhos/cm and 1 μS/cm = 1 μmhos/cm

Principle

The quantity and kind of ions present in a solution affect conductivity, which is a numerical representation of a water sample's capacity to conduct electricity. Since the majority of dissolved inorganic compounds in water are ionised, they add to conductance. The definition of conductance G is the reciprocal of resistance R.

$$G = \frac{1}{R}$$

A solution's conductance is measured between two chemically inert electrodes that are anchored in space. An alternating current signal is used to measure conductance in order to prevent polarisation at the electrode surface. The solution's conductance (G) is directly proportional to the surface area (A, cm^2) and inversely proportional to length between the electrode (L, cm). The constant of proportionality (K) also called conductivity (specific conductance).

$$G = K\frac{A}{L}$$

The unit of K is mho per centimeter. Conductivity is defined as conductance of a conductor 1 cm in length and 1 cm^2in cross-sectional area. Nature of the

Conductor (solution between the electrodes), pressure and ion concentrations are determining the conductivity.

The solution's conductance measure by conductivity cell which is depends on cell parameters, A and L. Although theoretically one could calculate the specific conductance from measurements of G (or R) and values of A and L as

Specific conductance, k = G × Kc

Where, K_c is equal to L/A and is known as the cell constant. Typical values of cell constant ranged from 0.10 to 2 cm^{-1}.

The cell constant ($K_c cm^{-1}$) is calculated as follows:

$$Kc = \frac{\text{Conductivity of standard KCL solution, } \mu\text{mhos / cm}}{\text{meter conductance}}$$

Apparatus

Electrical conductivity meter

Reagents

Standard potassium chloride, (0.01M): Dissolve 372.8 mg anhydrous KCl in distilled water or deionized water and make up to 500 ml. This standard solution at 25 °C has a specific conductance 1412 µmhos/cm.

Procedure

The conductivity should be measure in the field or in the laboratory as soon as water sample collected. Conductivity is depend on temperature, the water sample's essential to measure and noted if the conductivity is not an automatic temperature correction feature.

7

Salinity

The total amount of salts dissolved in water is known as salinity. Salinity of water is denoted as ppt, g/L, psu. Salinity of different water has been classified as Freshwater 0-0.5 ppt, Brackish water 0.5-30ppt and Marine water > 300 ppt.

Reagents

1. Silver nitrate ($AgNO_3$) (0.1N): Dissolve 4.25 g silver nitrate in distilled water and make the total volume 250 ml by shaking.
2. Potassium chromate (K_2CrO_4) indicator (5%): Dissolve 2.5 g potassium chromate in distilled water and make the total volume 50 ml by shaking.

Procedure

1. Salinity in estuarine and coastal water can be estimated by this method.
2. Take 10 ml of water sample in a 50 ml conical flask.
3. Add 3-4 drops of potassium nitrate indicator solution to it.
4. Titrate against 0.1N Silver nitrate till the yellow colour changes to brick red.

Calculation

Salinity (in ppt or g/L) = 0.03 + 1.805 ×chlorinity

Chlorinity (ppt or g/L) = Volume of 0.1 N silver nitrate

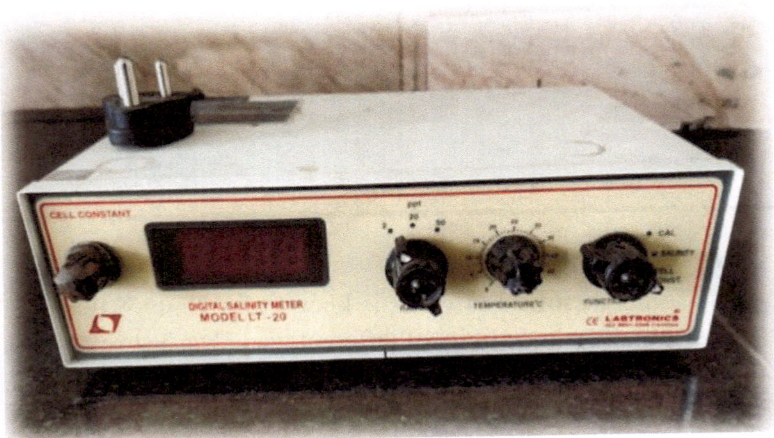

Fig. Digital Salinity meter

- For example, after titration 5 ml 0.1N silver nitrate used then chlorinity will be 5 g/l

Then salinity = 0.03+1.805 × 5

Salinity = 9.175g/l or ppt

8

Turbidity (Nephelometric Method)

The decreased ability of water to transmit light which is caused by suspended particulate matter ranging in size from colloidal to coarse dispersions is refers as turbidity.

Principle

Turbidity is measured by its effect on the transmission of light, which is termed as Turbidimetry or by its effect on the scattering of light, which is termed as Nephelometry. Turbidimeter can be used for sample with moderate turbidity and Nephelometer for samples with low Turbidity. Higher the intensity of scattered light higher the turbidity.

1 mg SiO_2/L = 1 unit of turbidity

Apparatus

Nephelopmeter: range 0.05 - 40 NTU

Reagents

Formazine Turbidity Suspension, Stock: Under strictly regulated circumstances, hydrazine sulphate and hexamethylenetetramine react to produce a stock turbidity suspension for formazine polymer.

a) **Solution I:** Dissolve 1gm hydrazine sulfate $(NH_2)_2\ H_2SO_4$ and dilute to make up 100 ml in volumetric flask.

b) **Solution II:** Take 10 gm hexamethylenetetramine and dilute and dilute to make up in 100 ml volumetric flask.

c) **Solution III:** Taking 5 ml of solution I and 5 ml of solution II and mix both solution and keep solution to stand for 24 h at 25 to 28°C and dilute to 100 ml mix 5 ml of solution –I with 5 ml of solution- II. Allow to stand for 24h at 25 to 28°C and dilute to 100 ml after reaction. This mixed solution will have turbidity of 400 units (NTU). This 400 NTU has to be prepared monthly.

1. Formazine turbidity suspension, standard (40 NTU): Pipet 10 mL of 400 NTU stock into a 100-mL volumetric flask and dilute to 100 mL with

water. The turbidity of this suspension is defined as 40 NTU and has to be prepared weekly.

2. Diluted Formazine turbidity suspension, standard: Prepare diluted turbidity suspension below
3. NTU daily. Those above 4 NTU have a useful life of one week.

Procedure

1. Preparation of calibration curve: Prepare turbidity solution from 0 to 10 NTU as follows:

Stock turbidity solution 40 NTU. mL	Distilled water, mL	Total volume. mL	NTU
2.50	97.50	100	1
5.00	95.00	100	2
10.0	90.00	100	4
12.5	87.50	100	5
15.0	85.00	100	6
20.0	80.00	100	8
25.0	75.00	100	10

2. Calibration of instruments
3. Turbidity measurement of sample: Gently agitate the sample and wait till all air bubbles disappear.
4. The Nephelometer reading is noted and NTU value is determined from the standard curve

9

Dissolved Oxygen (DO)

Dissolved oxygen (DO) refers to oxygen gas that is dissolved in water. Fish are able to absorb oxygen directly from the water into their bloodstream using gills. There are three main sources of oxygen in the aquatic environment: 1) direct diffusion from the atmosphere; 2) wind and wave action; and 3) photosynthesis. Oxygen depletion refers to low levels of DO and may result in fish mortality. A concentration of 5 mg/L DO is recommended for optimum fish health. Sensitivity to low levels of dissolved oxygen is species specific, however, most species of fish are distressed when DO falls to 2-4 mg/L. Mortality usually occurs at concentrations less than 2 mg/L. If fishes gulfing on the water surface and also show the low swimming in the water it indicates deficiency of dissolved oxygen in pond.

Diurnal changes of DO

Morning	5.0-7.0 mg/l	Lower due to overnight respiration
Afternoon	6.0-9.0 mg/l	Higher due to photosynthesis
Evening	5.0-7.0 mg/l	Gradually decline
Night	3.0-5.0 mg/l	Lowest point

Principle (azide modification)

Oxygen present in the sample oxidizes the divalent manganese to its higher valency, which precipitates as brown-hydrated oxides after addition of NaOH and KI. Upon acidification, manganese reverts to divalent state and liberates iodine from KI equivalent to DO content in the sample. The liberated iodine is titrated against $Na_2S_2O_3$) (N/80) using starch as an indicator. The series of reactions, which take place, can be summarized by the following equations.

$$MnSO_4 + 2NaOH \rightarrow Mn(OH)_2 \quad \text{(white ppt)} + Na_2SO_4$$

If no oxygen is present, a pure white precipitate of $Mn(OH)_2$ forms when $MnSO_4$ and alkali-iodide reagents (NaOH+ Kl) are added to the sample. If oxygen is present, the divalent Mn (II) is oxidised to higher valency Mn(IV) (i.e. MnO_2) and precipitate as a brown hydrated oxide.

$$Mn^{2+} + 2OH^- + {}^{1/2}O_2 \rightarrow MnO_2 \quad \text{(brown ppt)} + H_2O_3\text{, or}$$

$Mn(OH)_2 + 1/2O_2 \rightarrow MnO_2 + H_2O$

The oxidation of Mn(II) to MnO_2 sometimes, called fixation of the oxygen. Under acid condition MnO_2 reverts to divalent state by oxidising KI to produce I_2, which is liberated in solution.

$MnO_2 + 2I^- + 4H^+ \rightarrow Mn_2^+ + I_2 + 2\ H_2O$

The liberated free I_2 is titrated against standard solution of $Na_2S_2O_3$.

$Na_2S_2O_3 + I_2 \rightarrow 2NaI + Na_2S_4O_6$

Chemicals

1. Monohydrate manganous sulfate ($MnSO_4$)
2. Potassium iodide (KI) or sodium iodide (NaI)
3. Conc. H_2SO_4
4. Sodium thiosulfate ($Na_2S_2O_3$)
5. Potassium dichromate $K_2Cr_2O_7$)
6. Sodium hydroxide (NaOH)
7. Sodium azide (NaN_3)
8. Starch powder

Reagents

1. Manganous sulfate solution (364g/L): Dissolve 364 g of monohydrate manganous sulfate
2. (MnSO4.H_2O) in distilled water (filter it, if necessary) and dilute to 1L.
3. Alkaline-iodide-azide solution: Dissolve 500 g of NaOH and 150 g of KI (or 135g NaI) and dilute to 950 mL. Add 10g of sodium azide (NaN_3) dissolved in 40 mL of distilled water. Cool the solution and make up the volume to 1000 mL.
4. Standard sodium thiosulfate solution (0.025N): Dissolve directly 6.025 g $Na_2S_2O_3.5H_2O$ in a previously boiled 1 L cooled distilled water, which will give 0.025N. Add 1.5 mL 6N NaOH or 0.4 g solid NaOH per 1 L. Store in brown bottle.
5. Starch indicator: To prepare an aqueous solution take 5g of arrowroot or soluble starch to approximately 800 mL of boiling water, with stirring. Dilute to 1 L, boil a few minutes, and leave overnight. Use clear supernatant. Preserve by adding a few drops of toluene or formalin. Store in a glass-stoppered bottle.

Procedure

1. Collect the sample in a BOD bottle (300 mL capacity) taking care to avoid any bubbling. Fill the sample to the neck of the bottle. Be sure that air bubbles have not been trapped under the stopper and maintain a water seal around the stopper until ready for the next step of analysis.
2. Add 1 or 2 mL of manganous sulphate followed by 1 or 2 mL of alkali-iodide-azide solution. The tip of the pipette should be below the liquid level while adding these reagents.
3. Place the stopper carefully to exclude air bubbles and mix by inverting the bottle repeatedly for at least 15 minutes. An equivalent amount of 2 mL of the contents will come out of the bottle after placing the stopper.
4. Carefully remove the stopper and immediately add 1 or 2 mL of conc. H_2SO_4, close the bottle and mix with gentle inversion until the precipitate completely dissolves.
5. Titrate 50 or100 mL sample in the conical flask with sodium thiosulphate solution using 3-5 drops starch as an indicator. At the end point the blue colour turns to colourless.

Standardisation of sodium thiosulfate

It can be done either by standard bi-iodate solution or standard potassium dichromate solution.

1. Add 2g KI and 150 mL distilled water in a 500 mL conical flask.
2. Add few drops of conc. H_2SO_4 and 20 mL of 0.025N $K_2Cr_2O_7$
4. Dilute to 200 mL with distilled water. Keep in dark for 5 min.
5. The liberated iodine is titrated with sodium thiosulfate solution (0.025 N approx.), adding starch indicator towards the end of titration, when a pale straw color is reached.

$$\text{Normality of thiosulfate} = \frac{20 \times 0.025}{\text{mL of sodium thiosulfate}}$$

Calculation

When only a part of the sample of the content is titrated, i.e. 100 or 250 mL

$$\text{DO in mg / L} = \frac{\text{mL of titrant} \times \text{Normality} \times 8 \times 1000}{\text{V2}(\text{V1} - \text{v})\text{V1}}$$

Where,

V_1 =Volume of BOD bottle, mL

V_2= Volume of the contents titrated, Ml

8 = Millie equivalent weight of oxygen

v = Volume of $MnSO_4$ and iodide azide added, i.e. 1 + 1 = 2 mL

Fig. Pictorial representation of analysis of Dissolved Oxygen

For example

V= 20ml

N= 1/80

Vs= 300 ml

V1= 2 ml

Then

DO (mg/ml)= (20 x 1/80 x 800)/ (300 – 2)

DO = 2000/298

DO = 6.711 mg/ml

10

Biological Oxygen Demand (BOD)

The biochemical oxygen demand is a chemical procedure for determining the amount of dissolved oxygen needed by aerobic organisms in a water body to break the organic materials present in the given water sample at certain temperature over a specific period of time. BOD of water or polluted water is the amount of oxygen required for the biological decomposition of dissolved organic matter to occur under standard condition at a standardized time and temperature. Usually, the time is taken as 5 days and the temperature is 20°C.

$$C_6H_{12}O_6 + 6O_2 \xrightarrow{\text{microbes}} CO_2 + H_2O$$

Principle

The test measures the molecular oxygen utilized during a specified incubation period for the biochemical degradation of organic material (carbonaceous demand) and the oxygen used to oxidize inorganic material such as sulfides and ferrous ion. It also may measure the amount of oxygen used to oxidize reduced forms of nitrogen (nitrogenous demand).

Procedure

Fill two BOD bottles with sample (or diluted sample); the bottles should be completely filled.

Collect the water sample in BOD bottle

Determine initial DO (DOi) shortly after dilution is made; all oxygen uptake occurring after this measurement is included in the BOD measurement in one bottle immediately after filling with sample (or diluted sample),

it is usually necessary to dilute the sample to keep final DO above zero.

If during the five days of experiment, the DO drops to zero, then the test is invalid since more oxygen would have been removed had more been available.

The five-day BOD of a diluted sample is given by

$BOD_5 = [DOi - DOf] \times D.F.$ .... (1)

$BODm \times Vm = BODw \times Vw + BODd \times Vd$ ....(2)

Where,

BODm, is the BOD of the mixture of pond (wastewater) and dilution water BODd is the BOD of the dilution water alone;

Vw and Vd are the volumes of pond (wastewater) and dilution water respectively in the mixture

Vm= Vw+ Vd

Keep the other bottle in dark at 20°C for 5-days and determine DO (DOf) in the sample. Dissolved oxygen (DO) is determined according to the following procedure:

1. Add 1 mL of manganous sulfate solution to the BOD bottle by means of pipette, dipping in end of the pipette just below the surface of the water.
2. Add 1 mL of alkaline potassium iodide solution to the BOD bottle in a same way.
3. Insert the stopper and mix by inverting the bottle several times.
4. Allow the "precipitates" to settle halfway and mix again.
5. Again allow the "precipitates" to settle halfway.
6. Add 1 mL of concentrated sulfuric acid. Immediately insert the stopper and mix as before.
7. Allow the solution to stand at least 5 minutes.
8. Withdraw 100 mL of solution into an Erlenmeyer flask and immediately add 0.025N sodium thiosulfate drop by drop from a burette until the yellow color almost disappears.
9. Add about 1 mL of starch solution and
10. Titrate with thiosulfate solution until the blue color just disappears.
11. Record the ml. of thiosulfate solution used

Calculation

Calculating the five days BOD of diluted sample using the given formula

$BOD_5 = (DOI - DOF) \times D.F$

$BODm \times Vm = BODw \times Vw + BODd \times Vd$

Where, BODm = is the BOD of the mixture of pond (waste water) and dilution water.

BODd is the BOD of the dilution alone.

DOi- initial dissolve oxygen.

DOF- final dissolve oxygen.

D.F- dilution factor.

Vm- mixture volume.

Vw- volume of waste water.

Vd- volume of dilution water.

D.F= Vm/Vw

Formula BOD5= (DOI-DOF) × D.F

1. D.F= Vm/Vw

   Example, Vm= 300ml, Vw= 3ml, then

   D.F= 300/3

   D.F= 100
2. For example, DOI= mg/l and DOF= 2 mg/l
3. BOD5= (DOI-DOF) × D.F

   = (8-2) × 100

   BOD5= 600mg/l

Ideal BOD

Waste water fish culture	10-20 mg/l
Fresh water aquaculture pond	Below 3mg/l
Good and healthy aquatic life	1-2 mg/l
Poor water quality, fish stress and mortality	Above 5mg/l

- Range fresh water 1-5 mg/l
- Range brackish water 1-4 mg/l
- Marine water range <2mg/l

11

Free Carbon Dioxide (CO_2)

Free carbon dioxide in the water accumulates due to microbial activity and respiration of organisms. Surface waters normally contain less than 10 mg free CO_2 per litre while some groundwater may easily exceed that concentration up to 30 to 50 mg/L.

Principle

Free CO_2 reacts with sodium carbonate to form sodium bicarbonate, or with sodium hydroxide to form sodium carbonate. Completion of reaction is indicated by the development of the pink colour characteristics of phenolphthalein indicator at the equivalence pH of 8.3.

Analysis of Water and Effluents

$CO_2 + N_2CO_3 + H_2O = 2NaHCO_3$

$CO_2 + 2\ NaOH = N_2CO_3 + H_2O$

Reagents

1. Standard sodium hydroxide titrant (0.05N): Dissolve 40g of NaOH in boiled CO_2 free distilled water and make up the volume to 1 litre. Filter the solution through a sintered glass filter to remove any Na_2CO_3, the concentration of solution is 1N NaOH. Store it in in glass bottle.
2. Phenolphthalein indicator

Procedure

1. Take 50 ml of water sample in a conical flask and add 3-4 drops of phenolphthalein indicator
2. After adding 3-4 drops indicator, the water colour change to pink, it indicates no free CO_2 presence in water sample
3. If the water sample remain colour less after adding phenolphthalein indicator then it indicates presence of free CO_2 and water sample should titrate with NaOH 0.05 N until the pink colour appear.

Calculation

$$\text{Free } CO_2, (mg/L) = \frac{A \times N \times 44 \times 1000}{\text{ml sample}}$$

Where,

A = ml of titrant consume

N = normality of NaOH (0.05)

For example, if volume of water sample = 50ml

Volume of titrant consumed= 0.4 ml

Normality of NaOH is 0.05

So Free CO2 (mg/ml) = 0.4×0.05×44×1000/50

Free CO2 mg/l= 17.6

12

Chemical Oxygen Demand (COD)

Chemical oxygen demand (COD) is measurement of oxygen demand of waste in terms of the total quantity of oxygen required for oxidation of the waste to carbon dioxide and water. This test is based on the fact that all the organic compounds, with few exceptions, can be oxidized

The test is based on the fact that all organic compounds, with a few exceptions, can be oxidized by the action of strong oxidizing agents under acid conditions.

Organic matter + Oxidizing agent = $CO_2 + H_2O$.

The major advantage of COD test is the short time required for evaluation. The determination can be made in about 3 hours rather than the 5-days required for the measurement of BOD

Principle

The oxidizing agents like potassium permanganate and potassium dichromate is usually used to determine COD. Potassium permanganate is selective in the reaction like it reacts with carbonaceous on the other hand it shows non-reactive with nitrogenous matter.

Estimating of COD with any method, oxidizing agent must be present to ensure that organic matter is oxidized completely. The organic matter and oxidisable inorganic substances present in water or wastewater get oxidised completely by standard potassium dichromate ($K_2Cr_2O_7$) in the presence of H_2SO_4 to produce $CO_2 + H_2O$.The excess $K_2Cr_2O_7$ remaining after the reaction is titrated with ferrous ammonium sulphate $[Fe(NH_4)_2(SO_4)_2]$. The dichromate consumed gives the 02 required for oxidation of the organic matter.

$2\ K_2Cr_2O_7 + 8H_2SO_4 \rightarrow 2K_2SO_4 + 2Cr_2(SO_4)_3 + 8H_2O + 3O_2$

$C_6H_{12}O_6 + 6O_2 \rightarrow 6CO_2 + 6H_2O$

This requires that equitably excess present in all samples. Hence, for analysis the excess in some manner so that the real amount can be estimate. Usually a solution of a reducing agent (containing ammonium oxalate) is utilized for this purpose.

An excess of $K_2Cr_2O_7$ must be present in COD analysis. Thus excess added and actual amount reduced is determined. Ferrous ammonium sulfate is used for back titration.

Apparatus

1. A heating plate
2. COD reflux apparatus

Chemicals

1. Potassium dichromate, $K_2Cr_2O_7$
2. Conc. sulphuric acid, H_2SO_4(sp. gr. = 1.84)
3. Sulphamic acid
5. Silver sulfate, Ag_2SO_4
6. Ferrous ammonium sulfate, $Fe(NH_4)_2(SO_4)_2.6H_2O$
7. Mercuric sulfate, $HgSO_4$

Reagents

1. Standard potassium dichromate ($K_2Cr_2O_7$) solution (0.025N or 0.0417 M): Take 12.259 g of $K_2Cr_2O_7$ and dissolve in 1000 ml of distilled water. Then add 120 mg of sulphamic acid to take care of 6 mg/L of NO_2-N.
2. Standard $K_2Cr_2O_7$ solution, 0.025N: dilute 100 ml of 0.025 N $K_2Cr_2O_7$ solution to 1000 ml of distilled or deionized water (This solution is only if COD is estimated in the range of 10 to 50 mg/L).
3. Sulphuric acid (H_2SO_4) – silver sulphate reagent :Take 10 g of Ag_2SO_4 and add it to 1000 ml of H_2SO_4 and keep overnight for dissolution.
4. Standard ferrous ammonium sulphate (FAS), 0.25 N: dissolve 98 g of Ferrous ammonium sulfate, $Fe(NH_4)_2(SO_4)_2.6H_2O$in approx. 400 ml of deionized or distilled water and add 20 ml of conc. H_2SO_4cool and dilute to 1000 ml. Regular or daily standardize the solution against the standard $K_2Cr_2O_7$.

***Standard ferrous ammonium sulphate (FAS)**

Take 10 ml of Standard ferrous ammonium sulphate and dilute it to 100 ml of deionized or distilled water then acidify by 10 ml of H_2SO_4 and cool. Using 2-3 drops of ferroin indicator and titrate with ferrous ammonium sulfate.

Calculate normality as:

$$N = \frac{A \times B}{C}$$

Where,

N = Normality of FAS solution

A = Volume of potassium dichromate, ml

B = Normality of potassium dichromate solution

C = Volume of ferrous ammonium sulfate (FAS), ml

5. Standard ferrous ammonium sulfate 0.025 N: dissolved 9.8 g of Ferrous ammonium sulfate in 1000 ml of deionized or distilled water with 20 ml conc. sulphuric acid or dilute 100 ml of standard Ferrous ammonium sulfate (0.25 N) to 1000 ml.

Procedure

1. Take a flat bottom conical flask volume of 500 ml add 0.4 g of $HgSO_4$
2. Add 20 ml aliquot of sample diluted to 20 ml with distilled water, mix properly.
3. Add 10 ml potassium dichromate $K_2Cr_2O_7$ 0.025N or 0.25.
4. Slowly add 30 ml conc. H_2SO_4+ $AgSO_4$ reagent and mix properly. The slow addition of reagents swirling prevents fatty acids to escape out due to high temperature.
5. If the colour turns green after proper mixing then take sample and add more dichromate ($Cr_2O_7^{2-}$) and H_2SO_4, connect the conical flask to condenser then mix the contents properly before heating. Improper mixing may result in the form of bumping and sample will be blown out.
6. Reflux for a minimum of 2 h. Cool and then wash down the condenser with distilled water.
7. Dilute for a minimum of 150 ml (about 300 ml), cool to room temperature and titrate excess $K_2Cr_2O_7$ remaining after refluxing with corresponding standard ferrous ammonium sulfate using ferroin as an indicator (8-10 drops). Sharp color change from blue green to wine red indicates the end point or completion of titration.
8. Perform blank in the same manner using distilled water instead or sample

Calculation

$$\text{COD in mg / L} = \frac{\text{A - B} \times \text{N} \times 8 \times 1000}{\text{ml of the sample}}$$

Where,

A = Ferrous ammonium sulfate (ml) used for blank

B = Ferrous ammonium sulfate (ml) used for blank

N = Normality of ferrous ammonium sulfate

8 = Millie equivalent weight of oxygen

For example, if A= 15 ml

B= 5ml

N= 0.25

ml of sample used 500 ml

COD mg/l= (15-5) × 0.25×8×1000/500

COD mg/l= 40

13

Alkalinity

Principle

Alkalinity of a water sample is can be determined by titrating with standard sulphuric acid. Titration to pH 8.3 or de-colourization of phenolphthalein indicator will indicate complete neutralization of OH and ½ of CO_3 while to pH 4.5 or sharp change from yellow to pink of methyl orange indicator, that will indicate total alkalinity (complete neutralization of OH, CO_3, HCO_3)

Chemicals

1. Phenoplthalein indicator
2. Methyl orange indicator
3. Sodium carbonate, Na_2CO_3
4. Sodium hydroxide, NaOH
5. Sulphuric acid, H_2SO_4

Reagents

1. Phenolphthalein indicator: Dissolve 0.5 g in 500 ml 95% ethyl alcohol.
2. Methyl orange indicator: Dissolve 0.5 g of methyl orange in 100 ml of water and dilute to 1000 ml in deionized or distilled water (CO_2 free deionized or distilled water should be use).
3. Standard Sulphuric acid, H_2SO_4 (0.02N): to prepare 0.1N H_2SO_4 take 3 ml conc. H_2SO_4 and dilute it in to 1000 ml of deionized or distilled water. Standardise it against standard Na_2CO_3.
4. Sodium carbonate, Na_2CO_3 (0.05 N): Take 7g standard Sodium carbonate (Na_2CO_3) dry at 250 °C for 4 hr and cool in desicator then weigh 5.3 g and transfer it a 1000 ml volumetric flask after that fill to mark with distilled water. Solution should be use within 1 week.

Procedure

1. Take 50 ml sample in a 100 ml volume of conical flask then add 2- 3 drops of phenolphthalein indicator. If no color appears in water sample then the phenolphthalein alkalinity is zero.

2. If pink colour appears then titrate with H_2SO_4 0.02 N, till it disappears.
3. Add 2 to 3 drops of methyl orange in the same flask, then again titrate with H_2SO_4 till orange colour changes to pink.
4. If pink color does not appear in step 3 after addition phenolphthalein, continue as in (3) above.
5. Calculation of phenolphthalein and methyl orange alkalinity as follows and express in mg /L as $CaCO_3$

- After addition of phenolphthalein indicator if there is no any colour appeared phenolphthalein alkalinity = 0
- If pink colour appears after adding phenolphthalein indicator → titrate → pink to colourless (endpoint) → A
- After adding methyl orange indicator → titrate → orange to pink (end point) → B

Calculation

- Phenolphthalein alkalinity (mg/l as $CaCO_3$) = (A × 1000) + ml sample
- Methyl orange alkalinity (mg/l as $CaCO_3$) = (B × 1000) + ml sample
- Total alkalinity (mg/L as $CaCO_3$) = [(A + B) ×1000] + mL sample

In case H_2SO_4 is not 0.02 N, apply the following formula:

$$\text{Alkalinity mg / L} = \frac{\text{A} \times \text{Normal} \times 50 \times 1000}{\text{ml of sample}}$$

For example, if volume of sample used 50 ml

A total volume of 0.02N H_2SO_4 Consumed 7.8 ml

Alkalinity mg/ml= 7.8×0.02×50×1000/50

Alkalinity mg/ml= 156

14

Calcium Hardness

Common elements of natural water that significantly contribute to its hardness include calcium and magnesium ions of these elements leached from rocks. Water hardness reduces the utility of water for domestic use. Calcium hardness sometimes may be helpful because it provides a coating in the pipes which protects them against corrosion.

Principle

When calcium and magnesium are present in the water, EDTA reacts with calcium first. EDTA can be used to directly measure calcium when the pH is raised to a point where magnesium hydroxide is mostly precipitated and an indicator that only combines with calcium is employed. At a pH of 12 to 13, several indicators change colour to indicate that all of the Ca has been incorporated by the EDTA. The variations between an aliquot titrated at pH 10 and one titrated at pH 12 or 13 are what define the amount of magnesium.

Reagents

1. **Sodium hydroxide solution, (80 g/L) 8%:** Dissolve 80 g of NaOH in distilled water to prepare 1000 mL of solution.
2. **Murexide (ammonium purpurate) indicator:** Take 100 g sodium chloride (NaCl) and 0.2 g of ammonium purpurate mix and grind together thoroughly to the fine powder (i.e. one that passes through a 40-mesh sieve) It changes the colour from pink to purple
3. **EDTA solution (0.01 M):** Dissolve 372.24 g of EDTA in 1000 ml of distilled water to form 1 M.

0.1M – 37.224g/1000ml

0.01M- 3.722g/1000ml

1 ml = 0.243 mg Mg; 1 ml = 0.401 mg Ca

Procedure

1. Take 50 mL of sample in a conical flask.

2. Take 1 ml sodium hydroxide (NaOH) and add to increase pH to 12.0 then a pinch of murexide indicator (0.1 to 0.2 mg) or 1-2 drops of indicator solution (After addition of NaOH titration should be completed within 5 minutes).
3. Titrate immediate against EDTA solution till pink colour changes to purple colour. 4. Run blank reagent with distilled water. Note the ml of EDTA required and keep it aside to compare endpoints of the sample titration.

Calculation

$$\text{Calcium hardness as } CaCO_3 \text{ (mg / L)} = \frac{T \times 1000 \times 1.05}{V}$$

Where,

T = volume of titrant, mL

V = volume of sample, mL

1.05 is a correction factor

For example, 50 ml water sample used and titrant used 6 ml of 0.01 M EDTA.

1. Calcium (mg/l) = (6×400.5×1.05)/50
   = 50.46 mg/l
2. Calcium hardness as CaCO3
   = (6×1000×1.05)/50
   =126 mg/l

15

Total Hardness

Hardness is the total soluble Ca and Mg Salts (in same cases Fe salts). It includes sulphates and chlorides along with carbonate, bicarbonate and hydroxide salts. Soft water: 0-100 mg/L, Hard water: 100 - 300 mg/L, Very hard water: > 300 mg/L CaCO3. Total hardness should be 50- 300 mg/L. Very hard water causes osmoregulatory stress to fish. Hardness below 50 mg/L reduces growth of plankton.

Reagents

1. 10.01M EDTA solution: Dissolve 3.72 g disodium salt of EDTA in distilled water and make the volume 1L by shaking.
2. Eriochrome Black T (EBT) Indicator: Add 0.2 g dry Eriochrome powder to 50 ml of triethyl amine. Add 5 ml absolute alcohol and shake it.
3. Ammonium chloride-Ammonium hydroxide buffer solution: Dissolve 17.5g ammonium chloride (NH_4Cl) in 142 ml of ammonia solution (NH_4OH). Add distilled water to make the volume 250 ml.

Procedure

1. Take 50ml water sample in a 250 ml conical flask.
2. Add 2 ml buffer solution and 5 drops of EBT indicator.
3. Wine-red colour will appear.
4. Titrate against 0.01M EDTA till the colour changes into bright greenish blue.

Calculation

$$\text{Total hardness} (\text{mg} / \text{L}\,\text{CaCO}_3) = \frac{\text{ml of } 0.01\text{M EDTA used in titration} \times 1000}{\text{Volume of sample ml}}$$

For example, 50ml water sample taken and 7.5 ml titrant was used

Then,

Total hardness mg/ml = $(7.5 \times 1000)/50$

=150 mg/ml

Ideal total hardness

Fresh water ponds	50-150 mg/l
Brackish water	75-200 mg/l
Marine water	100-250 mg/l

16

Chlorides

Principle

Chloride ion is determined by Mohr's method, titration with standard silver nitrate solution in which silver chloride is precipitated first. The end of titration is indicated by formation of red silver chromate from excess $AgNO_3$ and potassium chromate used as an indicator in neutral to slightly alkaline solution.

$AgNO_3 + Cl^- \rightarrow AgCl + NO_3$

$2AgNO_3 + K_2CrO_4 \rightarrow Ag_2CrO_4 + 2KNO_3$ (Reddish Brown)

Reagents

1. Standard Silver nitrate 0.0141N : Take 1.189 g and dissolved it in 500 ml distilled water.
2. Sodium chloride 0.014N: Dissolve 0.28 g sodium chloride in 500 ml of distilled water.
3. Potassium Chromate indicator

Procedure

1. Take 50 ml sample in a 100 ml conical flask
2. Adjust its pH in between 7.0 and 8.0 either with alkali or acid solution. Otherwise, AgOH is formed at high pH level or CrO_4^{-2} at low pH level.
3. Add 1 ml of potassium chromate (K_2CrO_4) colour turn to light yellow.
4. Titrate with standard silver nitrate ($AgNO_3$) solution till colour change from light yellow to brick red colour.
5. Note the volume of $AgNO_3$ added (A)
6. For better accuracy, titrate distilled water in the same manner
7. Note the volume of silver nitrate added for distilled water (B)

Calculation

$$\text{Chloride (mg/1)} = \frac{\text{A - B} \times 35.45 \times \text{N} \times 1000}{\text{Volume of sample ml}}$$

Where,

A=Volume of Silver Nitrate solution consumed in water sample (ml)

B= Volume of Silver Nitrate solution consumed in distilled water sample (ml)

N= Normality of $AgNO_3$

For example, if 50 ml sample were taken

Volume of Silver Nitrate solution consumed in water sample (ml) is 0.2 ml

Volume of Silver Nitrate solution consumed in distilled water sample (ml) is 0.1 ml

Normality of $AgNO_3$ is 0.0141

Then Chloride (mg/l) = [(0.2-0.1) x 35.45 x 0.0141 x 1000]/50

Chloride (mg/l) = 0.999

- The safe range for aquatic organism is 0.01-0.05

17

Ammonia

Fish excrete Ammonia, is a byproduct from protein metabolism and bacteria break down organic waste such as discarded food, faeces, dead planktons, sewage, and so on. When ammonia is unionized form (NH_3) is extremely dangerous; yet when ammonia ionized form (NH_4^+) it is harmless; both forms are known as total ammonia. Fish suffering from ammonia toxicity often"become lethargic and frequently emerge near the surface gasping for oxygen. common effects of ammonia in the range >0.1mg/l include Gill damage, breakdown of mucous-producing membranes, "sub-lethal" effects like reduced growth, poor (FC) feed conversion, and reduced disease resistance at concentrations lower than lethal concentrations, osmoregulatory imbalance, and kidney failure.

Principle

When Ammonia react with alkaline Nessler reagent (K_2HgI_4 or $2KI + HgI_2$) it produces a yellowish-brown coloured compound. Pretreatment with ZnSO4 and NaOH precipitates Ca, Mg, Fe and sulphide, which form turbidity and apparent colour. Addition of ethylene diamine tetraacetic acid, EDTA (before nessler's reagent) or Rochelle salt solution prevents precipitation of residual Ca and Mg in presence of the alkaline Nesslers's reagent.

$$2K_2\,HgI_4 + NH_3 + 3KOH \rightarrow \text{I-Hg-O-Hg-NH}_2 + 7KI + 2H_2O$$

(yellow-brown colour)

Apparatus

1. Spectrophotometer (use at 400-500 nm)
2. pH meter

Chemicals

1. Ammonium chloride
2. Potassium iodide , KI
3. Sodium hydroxide
4. EDTA
5. Rochelle salt (Potassium sodium tartrate tetra tetrahydrate)

6. Zinc sulfate
7. Mercuric iodide

Reagents

1. **Zinc sulfate solution:** Take 100 g of $ZnSO_4.7H_2O$, dissolved in distilled water and dilute to 100 ml.
2. **Sodium hydroxide, 6N:** Take 24 g of NaOH and dilute to 100 ml.
3. **EDTA reagent:** Dissolve 50 g of EDTA in 60 ml distilled water containing 10 g NaOH. Gentle heating is required to complete dissolution. Leave at room temperature for cool down and final volume in 100 ml volumetric flask.
4. **Rochelle salt solution:** Take 50g of Rochelle salt ($KNaC_4H_6O_6.H_2O$) in 100 ml of water. Remove NH_3 by boiling off 39 ml solution after cooling dilute to 100 ml.
5. **Nessler reagent:** Take 100g $HgCl_2$ and 70 g KI, dissolve in a small quantity of distilled water. Another solution is prepare by adding 160 g NaOH in 500 ml water, mix solution 1 and 2, dilute to 1000 ml. Keep it overnight. Filter through a glass fibre filter before using. Store supernatant in a coloured bottle
6. **Stock ammonia solution:** Dissolve 3.819 g anhydrous NH_4Cl, dried at 100°C and dilute to 1000 ml. 1 ml = 1 mg N= 1.22 mg NH_3
7. **Standard ammonia solution:** Dilute 10 ml of stock ammonia solution to 1 L with distilled water. 1 ml = 10 µg N= 12.2 µg NH_3

Procedure

1. Take 100 ml sample in an erlenmeyer flask or conical flask
2. Add 1 ml solution of $ZnSO_4$ and or 0.50 ml NaOH to obtain a pH of 10.5. Allow to settle and filter the supernatant through Whatman filter paper No. 42.
3. Take an aliquot of sample and dilute to 50 ml.
4. Add 3 drops of Rochelle salt solution or 1 drop of EDTA and mix well.
5. Add 3 ml Nesslers's reagent, if EDTA is used or add 1 ml Nesslers's reagent if Rochells salt solution is used and make up to 100 ml.
6. After mixing well read absorbance (optical density) after 10 minutes at 410 nm against a blank prepared in the same way using distilled water instead of sample.
7. Prepare a calibration curve using suitable aliquots of standard solution in the range of 5 to 120 µg/L 100 ml (0.5 to 1.2 mg/l). For reference

follow the same procedure as per steps 1 to 5 above, but use the standard solution in place of sample.

8. The value of ammonia is obtained from the standard graph and multiplied by the dilution factor.
    1. Sample= 100 ml
    2. Dilution- After treatment with zinc Sulphate & sodium hydroxide, an aliquot of 10 ml is taken & diluted to 50ml.

The absorbance of the diluted sample after adding Nasler's reagent is measured as 0.500 at 410 nm.

Where (NH_3) is the concentration of ammonia in µg/l

Calculation

NH_3= (0.500-0.02)/0.01

NH3= 48 µg/l

3. The 10 ml aliquot was diluted to 50 ml

   So the dilution factor is 50/10 = 5

   NH3 in original aliquot = 48 x 5 = 240 µg/l
4. Correct initial 100 ml sample volume & final 100ml Nessler's reagent the final volume is 100ml, while the aliquot is 50 ml, so the dilution factor is 100/50 = 2

NH3 = 240 x 2 = 480 µg/l or 0.48 mg/l.

- Ammonia level harmful to fish freshwater >0.05 mg/l.
- Ammonia range in marine water 0.02-0.4 ppm.
- Ammonia range in brackish water 0.05 mg/l

18

Nitrogen (Nitrite) (NO_2^-N)

Nitrite (NO_2^-) is formed in waters by oxidation of ammonia compounds (by aerobic nitrifying bacteria, e.g. Nitrosomonas) or by reduction of nitrate (by facultative anaerobic denitrifying bacteria, e.g. Pseudomonas). Such oxidation and reduction may occur in wastewater treatment plants, water distribution system, and natural waters. As an intermediate stage in nitrogen cycle, it is unstable. Very high nitrite levels are usually associated with waters having unsatisfactory microbiological activity.

Principle (Colorimetric method)

When nitrite (NO_2^-) as nitrous acid (HNO_2) mixes with sulfanilamide in an acidic environment (pH 2-2.5), a diazonium salt is created. This salt then combines with N-(1-naphthyl)-ethylenediamine dihydrochloride (NED dihydrochloride) to make a vivid pinkish red azo-dye. The amount of nitrite in the sample directly correlates with the colour that is created. At 543 nm, the colour follows Beer's law up to 180 µg/L with a 1 cm light path. By diluting a sample, a higher nitrite concentration can be determined.

Sulfanilamide + HNO_2 + HCl → Diazonium salt + H_2O.

Diazonium salt + NED-dihydrochloride → Red colouredazo dye.

Storage of sample

Acid preservation is not preferred for samples to be analysed for nitrite. For fresh samples stop bacterial conversion of nitrite to nitrate or ammonia, short-term preservation of 1 to 2 days, store at 4 °C

Apparatus

Spectrophotometer: at 543 nm

Chemicals

1. Sodium nitrite,
2. Sulfanilamide, KNO_2
3. Chloroform, CHC_{13}
4. N-(1-naphthyl)-ethylenediamine dihydrochloride (NED dihydrochloride)

5. Phosphoric acid, H_3PO_4, 85%
6. Conc. H_2SO_4

Procedure

1. Take 50 mL of sample in a 100 mL volumetric flask.
2. Removal of suspended solids: If sample contains suspended solids, filter it through Whatman no. 42 filter paper.
3. Check the pH of the solution. If pH is not between 5 to 9, neutralize pH by adding 1 N HCI, pH as required.
4. Add 2 mL of colour reagent, mix well and makeup the volume to 100 mL. At this stage pH should be 2-2.5.
5. Measure the colour after 10 min at 543 nm. Prepare calibration curve in the range of 0 to 1 mg NO_2-NIL at the interval of (1 mg NO_2 -NIL.).
6. Prepare a blank in the same way by using distilled water instead of the sample.
7. Calculate and record as NO_2 -N in mg/L.

Calculation

Read the concentration of NO_2-N in samples directly from the calibration curve.

If less than 50 mL of sample is taken, calculate the concentration as follows:

$$\text{Nitrite (as N), mg/L} = \frac{\text{mg/L from standard curve} \times 50}{\text{ml sample}}$$

For example, if value from standard curve is 0.006 mg/l and 20 ml sample taken then

Nitrite (as N), mg/l= 0.006 50/20 = 0.015 mg/l.

- Sub lethal level for fish is 0.02-1 mg/l, 1-10 is lethal and <0.02 is optimal for fish health

19

Nitrogen (Nitrate) (NO_3^-N)

The most oxidizable form of nitrogen is nitrate nitrogen (NO_3^-N), which is found in minimal amounts in surface waters but can reach considerable concentrations in some aquifers. An essential plant nutrient, nitrate also contributes to eutrophication in receiving water bodies.

Principle

Nitrate reacts with phenol disulphonic acid and produces a nitro-derivative which in alkaline solution develops yellow colour due to rearrangement of its structure. The yellow colour follows Beer's law and is proportional to the concentration of nitrate present in the sample. Ultraviolet (UV) technique measures the absorbance of nitrate at 220 nm, which is suitable for screening uncontaminated water (low in organic matter). A second measurement made at 275 nm, may be used to correct the nitrate value (because 275 nm is not absorbed by nitrate, but absorbed by other matter). The nitrate calibration curve follows Beer's law up to 11mg NO_3^-N /L.

Reagents

1. Stock nitrate solution (1ml=100 µg NO_3^-N): Dry potassium nitrate (KNO_3) in an oven at 105 °C for 24 h. Take 360.9 mg potassium nitrate and dissolve in distilled water and dilute to 500 ml. Preserve it with adding 1 ml of chloroform in per 500 ml stock nitrate solution. This solution will stable for at least 6 months.
2. Intermediate nitrate solution (1 ml = 10µg NO_3^-N): Take 100 ml of stock nitrate solution and dilute it to 1000 ml of distilled water. This solution can be preserve by adding 2 ml of chloroform per 1000 ml. This Intermediate nitrate solution will stable for at least 6 months.
3. Hydrochloric acid (HCL) solution, 1N: Take 83 ml of hydrochloric acid and dilute it to 1000 ml of distilled water.

Procedure

1. Take 50 ml of filtered sample, add 1 ml hydrocholoric acid solution in it and mix thoroughly

2. Preparation of standard curve Prepare nitrate calibration standards in the range 0- 7 mg/L. Dilute the following volumes of intermediate nitrate solution i.e., 0,1,2,4,7,10,15,20,25,30 and 35 ml to 50 ml with distilled water. Treat the standards in same manner as sample.
3. Spectrophotometeric reading Read absorbance against distilled water and set at zero absorbance. Use a wavelength ~ 220 nm to obtain NO_3^-N reading and a wavelength of ~ 275 nm to estimate interference due to dissolved organic matter.

Calculation

1. For samples and standards, subtract two times the absorbance reading at 275 nm from the reading at 220 nm to obtain absorbance due to NO_3^-N only.
2. Make a standard curve by plotting absorbance due to nitrate against NO_3^-N concentration.
3. Obtain sample concentration directly from the standard curve.

Note: If correction value is more than 10% of the reading at 220 nm, do not use this method.

20

Total Phosphorus

Phosphorus is nearly exclusive found as phosphates in waters and wastewater and it categorised in to: a) orthophosphate, (b) organically bound phosphate and (c) condensed phosphates. Theses all three forms of phosphorus occur in solution, in the body of aquatic organisms through food chain. All the forms of phosphorous, whether dissolved or particulate are converted to inorganic forms (phosphate) after digestion of sample. Various methods use for the digestion of the sample including use of perchloric acid, H_2SO_4- K_2SO_4, H_2SO_4- HNO_3 etc. The H_2SO_4- HNO_3 digestion technique is discussed here.

Reagents

1. Phenolphthalein indicator
2. Conc. sulphuric acid (H_2SO_4)
3. Conc. nitric acid (HNO_3)
4. Sodium hydroxide (NaOH), 1 N: Dissolve take 40 g of NaOH in 1000 ml of distilled water

Procedure

Digestion

1. Take 50 ml of sample in a Kjeldahl flask
2. Add 1 ml H_2SO_4 and 5 ml HNO_3
3. Once the HNO completely removed, digest the sample on a hot plate until the volume approaches 5 ml. Then, keep heating the solution until it loses colour (you may also heat it in a beaker covered with a watch glass to prevent excessive evaporation).

Estimation of Phosphorus

1. Completely cool and transfer sample to 100 ml volumetric flask.
2. Add 1 drop of phenolphthalein indicator
3. Neutralise the acidity by adding 1 N NaOH. At the solution pink. Make up the final volume to 100 ml.

Colour development

1. Take 20 ml of digested sample in an erlenmeyer flask and 4 ml of ammonium molybdate in it reagent I and 0.5 ml (10 drops) stannous chloride reagent II.
2. Temperature of the final solution affects both colour intensity and rate of colour development. A temperature increase of 1°C results in a 1% increase in colour. Because of this, keep the reagent, standards, and samples 2°C apart and in the 20–30°C temperature range.

Colour measurement

1. After 10 min, but before 12 min, measure the absorbance of the colour spectrometric at 690 nm and compare with a caliberation curve, using blank distilled water

Calculation,

$$\text{Phosphate, mg / L} = \frac{\text{mg of P (in approx..104.5 ml final volume}}{\text{ml sample}} \times 1000$$

- The P:N ratio for freshwater and brackish water should be 1:4.
- The total phosphorus level in freshwater & brackish water should not exceed 0.5 mg/l.

21

Sulphate

Sulfate can have harmful effects on aquatic life in freshwaters, sulfate cause osmotic stress or specific ion toxicity in aquatic organisms, especially in soft waters where Ca^{2+} and Mg^{2+} concentrations are low. Egg fertilization and early embryonic development were the most sensitive developmental stages of whitefish to sulfate (Karjalainen et al., 2021).

Sulphate (SO_4^{2-}) may be estimated by either turbidimetric or gravimetric methods (APHA, 1995)

1. Turbidimetric method is more applicable in the range of 1- 40 mg Sulphate (SO_4^{2-})/ L
2. Gravimetric method is suitable if the concentration of Sulphate (SO_4^{2-}) is above 10 mg/ L

Turbidimetric Method (Range 1 - 40 mg/L of sulphate)

Principle

Sulphate ion (SO_4^{2-}) precipitated with barium chloride ($BaCl_2$) in an acetic acid medium in order to form crystals of barium sulphate ($BaSO_4$).

$BaCl_2 + SO_4^{2-} + BaSO_4$ (precipitate)

The formation of these crystals is increased in the presence of an acetic acid solution containing sodium acetate, potassium nitrate, acetic acid and magnesium chloride. The suspended barium sulphate ($BaSO_4$) is measured by spectrophotometer and concentration of sulphate (SO_4^{2-}) is determined by comparison of the reading with a standard curve. Minimum detectable concentration is approximately 1 mg (SO_4^{2-}) / L.

Apparatus

1. Spectrophotometer (use at 420 nm)
2. Magnetic stirrer
3. Measuring spoon, capacity 0.2 to 0.3 mL
4. Stopwatch

Chemicals

1. Sodium acetate ($CH_3COONa.3H_2O$)
2. Magnesium chloride ($MgCl_2$. $6H_2O$)
3. Potassium nitrate (KNO_3)
4. Sodium sulphate (Na_2SO_4)
5. Barium chloride crystals ($BaCl_2$. $2H_2O$)
6. Acetic acid (CH_3COOH, 99%)

Reagents

1. **Buffer solution (A):** Take 1g potassium nitrate (KNO), 5g sodium acetate ($CH_3COONa.3H_2O$, 30g magnesium chloride ($MgCl6H_2O$), 20 mL acetic acid (CH_3COOH, 99%) and dissolve in 500 mL distilled water and make up to 1000 mL.
2. **Buffer solution (B) (required when the sulphate concentration is less than 10 mg/L):** Dissolve 30g magnesium chloride ($MgCl_2.6H_2O$), 5 g sodium acetate ($CH_3COONa.3H_2O$), 0.111g sodium sulphate (Na_2SO_4) and 20 mL acetic acid (CH_3COOH, 99%) in 500 mL of distilled water and make up to 1 L.
3. **Barium chloride, $BaCl_2.2H_2O$:** For the preparation of crystals of 20 to 30 mesh size in the laboratory, spread crystals over a large watch glass, desiccate for 24h. Remove any crystals that are not 20 to 30 mesh size. Store in a clean dry jar. Uniform standardisation turbidity is produced with this mesh range and the appropriate buffer.
4. **Standard sulphate solution:** Take 0.1479g anhydrous Na_2SO_4 & dissolve in distilled water diluting in 1000 ml. 1 ml = 100µg sulphate.

Procedure

1. Formation of barium sulphate turbidity
   - If the sample is turbid filter the sample and adjust the temperature between to 30°C
   - Take 100 ml sample into a 250 ml conical flask.
   - Add 20 ml buffer solution and mix properly in a stirring apparatus.
   - Stir for 60± 2 seconds at constant speed. Stirring should be at a constant rate in all determinations.
   - While stirring, add 0.3g of $BaCl_2$ crystrals and immediately note the timing
2. Measurement of barium sulphate turbidity

- After stirring, pour solution into absorption cell of photometer and measure the turbidity at 5 ± 0.5 min

3. Preperation of calibration curve
   - Estimate sulphate concentration in sample by comparing turbidity reading with a caliberation curve prepared by carrying sulphate standards through entire procedure
   - Standards at 5 mg/L increments in the 0 to 40 mg/L sulphate range.
   - $BaSO_4$ suspensions lose stability and above 40 mg/L accuracy decreases, check reliability of the caliberation curve by running a standard with every three or four samples.
4. Correction for sample colour and turbidity
   - Correct sample colour and turbidity by running blanks to which $BaCl_2$ is not added.

Calculation

$$SO_4^{2-}\ mg/1 = \frac{mg\,SO_4^{2}{-} \times 1000}{ml\,sample}$$

This formula calculates the concentration of Sulphate in milligram per liter based on the mass of Sulphate and volume of the sample.

For example, if MgSO4 in sample = 2 mg and sample volume 100ml.

Sulphate mg/l= (2/100) x 1000 = 20 mg/l.

22

Total Plate Count

The total plate count (TPC) is also called the Bacterial plate count (BPC), aerobic plate count, standard plate count (SPC), total viable count (TVC) or mesophilic count represents the number of colony forming units (CFU) per g (or per mL) of growing microorganisms such as bacteria, yeast and mold on a non-specific solid bacteriological growth medium under the specified conditions. Temperature, incubating time, medium type, and any other conditions used in the enumeration varies upon reference standards and laboratory objectives. Laboratories participating in the program choose their own routine conditions.

Principle

Usually direct count of too many bacteria in a sample is difficult but the bacterial colonies may be used as a measure of the bacterial cells in the known serially dilution and plated out on an agar surface in such a way that single isolated bacteria form visible isolated colonies. However, colony-forming unit might actually consist of a chain of bacteria rather than a single bacterium if the organism often develops various cell configurations, such chains. Furthermore, a portion of the bacteria might be grouped together. Thus, typically refer to the process of using the plate count technique as a means of estimating the number of colony forming units (CFUs) in that known solution. Then further this figure use to extrapolate the total amount of CFUs present in the original sample.

The bacterial sample is typically plated on agar after being diluted by a factor of 10 or as a requirement. The quantity of colonies on a dilution plate determined after incubation that shows between.

Equipment and Glassware

Autoclave, Balance, Colony counter, Test tubes/dilution bottles, Incubator, Microwave oven, Petri dish container, Petri dishes, Pipettes or Pipette aids Refrigerator, Sterilizing oven, Thermometer, Water bath etc.

Materials

- Nutrient agar/Luria-Bertani Agar
- Sterile Dilution blanks (containing 9 ml of 0.9% $NaCl_2$)

Dilution of samples

Fill blank water in to test tubes or dilution bottle each dilution tubes will contain 9 ml blank water.

Why use serial dilution

- Bacteria undergo exponential growth this many may be present in each sample
- In order to count the number of bacteria, each colony must be single and distinct
- The number of countable colonies per plate is 30-300
- Serial dilutions allow one to dilute a sample of bacteria to the point that the total number of bacteria to the point

Procedure

- Take the sample
- Label the test tubes of saline solution for serial dilution 10^{-1}, 10^{-2}, 10^{-3}, 10^{-4}, 10^{-5}, 10^{-6}......10^{-10}, Label the petri plates as labeled to test tubes 1-10.
- Using aseptic technique, the initial dilution is made by transferring 1 ml of water sample to a 9 ml sterile saline blank in to tubes 10^{-1}, 10^{-2}, 10^{-3}, 10^{-4},10^{-5} 10^{-6}......10^{-10}.
- The sterile saline blank is then shake properly by grasping the tube between the palms of both hands and rotating quickly to create a vortex or by using vortex machine to distribute the bacteria and break up any clumps.
- Transfer 1 ml of solution from tube 1 ml of solution from the tube 1 into tube 2 and mix gently then following this 1 ml of solution from the tube 2 into tube 3 and so on.
- Inoculate the samples in each poured petri plates labeled as 1-6 from the serially diluted samples 10^{-1}, 10^{-2}, 10^{-3}, 10^{-4}, 10^{-5} 10^{-6}.
- Inoculated plates further kept in bacteriological incubator on suitable temperature 30-37°C for 24 hours.
- At the end of the incubation period, select all of the petri plates containing between 30 and 300 colonies.

Calculation (Colony Forming Unit CFU)

$$\text{No. of colonies per ml of sample} = \frac{\text{no. of colonies} \times \text{dillution factor of the plate counted}}{\text{ml of sample plated}}$$

To calculate the total plate count (TPC) also known as the colony forming unit (CFU) per milliliter of sample.

For example, suppose after performing serial dilution & plating, the petriplate with a dilution of (10^{-3} 1/1000) has 150 colonies, & 0.1 ml of the diluted sample

1. Number of colonies 150

   Dilution factor 1000 (since the dilution is 10^{-3})

   Volume plated 0.1 ml

2. CFU/ml= (150 x 1000)/0.1

   CFU/ml= 150000/0.1 = 1500000

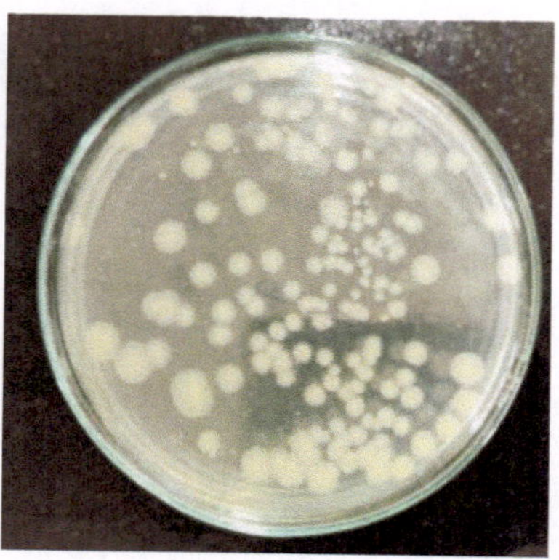

23

Pipettes

Laboratory pipettes are classified by their method of liquid transfer. There are two types of pipette one is plastic which is made up of polystyrene and are essentially disposable and second one is glass pipettes are very resistant to chemicals. Glass pipette can be used frequently by washing, sterilising and dry heat sterilisation is also available. Some of the common types of pipettes are using in laboratory such as serological, volumetric, micropipettes, multichannel, and Pasteur pipettes. Serological and graduated pipettes are used for transferring various volumes, while micropipettes and volumetric types of pipettes are only considered for precise measurement and transfer. Multichannel pipettes are used for dispensing into multiple wells, and Pasteur pipettes are simple for transferring small amounts.

1. **Serological Pipettes**
   - Also known as graduated pipettes, made of glass or transparent polystyrene they are calibrated with markings to measure and dispense varying volumes.
   - Appropriate for cell culture applications, transferring liquids and mixing.
2. **Multichannel Pipettes**
   - It is design to transfer multiple samples at once, often used for 96 well plates or pcr tubes.
   - It can be manual or automated, with multiple heads for faster dispensing.
3. **Volumetric Pipettes**
   - It is designed to supply for single and particular volume of liquid.
   - Marked by single graduation for an exact volume, such as 1, 5, 10, 25, and 50 mL.
   - Used in chemical reactions and analysis where accuracy is crucial.

4. **Pasteur Pipettes**
   - Disposable or reusable pipettes used for small amounts of liquids.
   - Generally made up of glass or plastic and have a rubber bulb for aspiration.
5. **Micropipettes**
   - Small, precision instruments used to measure and transfer very small volumes (e.g., microliters).
   - Often equipped with a plunger for drawing up and dispensing liquid.
   - Common in molecular biology, PCR, and cell culture.

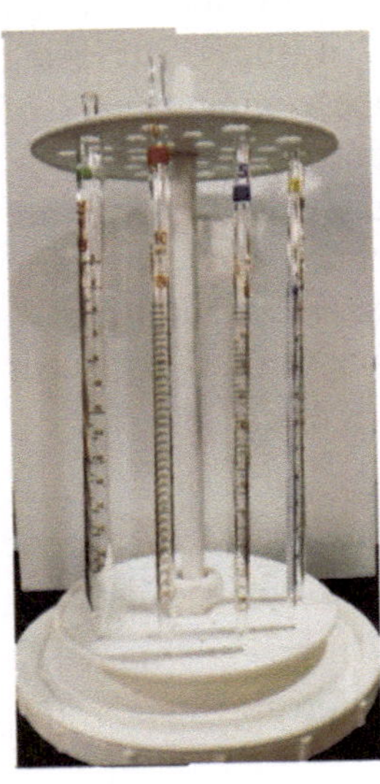

Serological pipettes

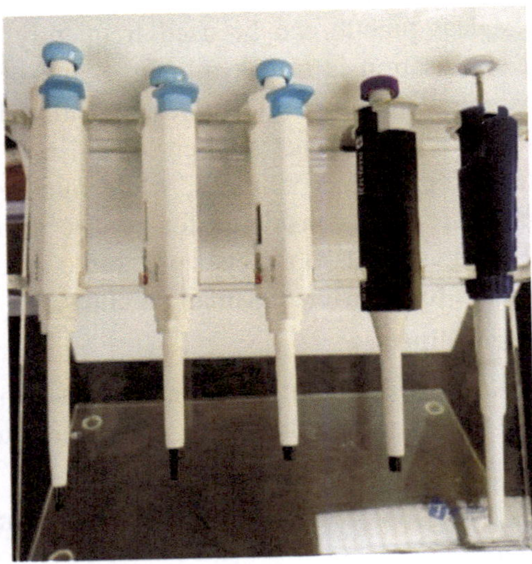

Micropipettes

Appendices

Appendix A: Ideal values of Physico-chemical parameters of water for freshwater Aquaculture

Sl. No.	Parameters	Standard value
1.	Colour	Clear water with greenish hues <100 colour units
2.	pH	6.7-8.5
3.	Transparency	20-25
4.	Total solids	<500
5.	Conductivity	100-2000μs/cm
6.	Salinity	<0.5
7.	Turbidity	25-30 cm (Secchi disc visibility)
8.	Dissolved oxygen	5-10
9.	Biological Oxygen Demand	<10
10.	Free CO_2	<3
11.	Chemical Oxygen Demand	<50
12.	Alkalinity	50-300
13.	Calcium Hardness	75-150
14.	Total Hardness	30-180
15.	Chlorides	31-50
16.	Ammonia	0-0.1
17.	Nitrite	0-0.5
18.	Nitrate	0.1-3
19.	Phosphate	0.05-0.4

Appendix B: Ideal values of Physico-chemical parameters of water for Carp Aquaculture

Sl. No.	Parameters	Standard value
1.	Temperature °C	27-32
2.	Dissolve oxygen (mg/l)	5.5-7.5
3.	Alkalinity (mg/l)	80-150
4.	Hardness(mg/l)	60-80
5.	pH	7.5-8.5
6.	Ammonia (mg/l)	0.05-0.1
7.	Nitrite (mg/l)	<0.02

Appendix C: Ideal value of Physico-chemical parameters of water for Catfish Aquaculture

Sl. No.	Parameters	Standard value
1.	Temperature °C	26-28
2.	Dissolve oxygen (mg/l)	4-6
3.	Alkalinity (mg/l)	75-200
4.	Hardness(mg/l)	70-150
5.	pH	6.5-7.5
6.	Ammonia (mg/l)	0.05-0.2
7.	Nitrite (mg/l)	<0.02

Appendix D: Ideal value of Physico-chemical parameters of water for Prawn Aquaculture

Sl. No.	Parameters	Standard value
1.	pH	7-8.5
2.	Water Temperature °C	28-31 °C
3.	Salinity (ppt)	11-15
4.	Dissolved Oxygen(mg/l)	5-8
5.	Total Alkalinity (mg/l)	100-150
6.	Ammonia (mg/l)	0.01-0.1

Appendix E: Ideal value of Physico-chemical parameters of water for Re-circulatory Aquaculture System

Sl. No.	Parameters	Standard value
1.	Temperature °C	25-30
2.	Dissolve oxygen (mg/l)	5-7
3.	Alkalinity (mg/l)	80-120
4.	Hardness(mg/l)	-
5.	pH	7.5-8.5
6.	Ammonia (mg/l)	<0.1
7.	Nitrite (mg/l)	<0.01

Annexure

Conical flask

Volumetric flask

Reagent bottles

Beaker

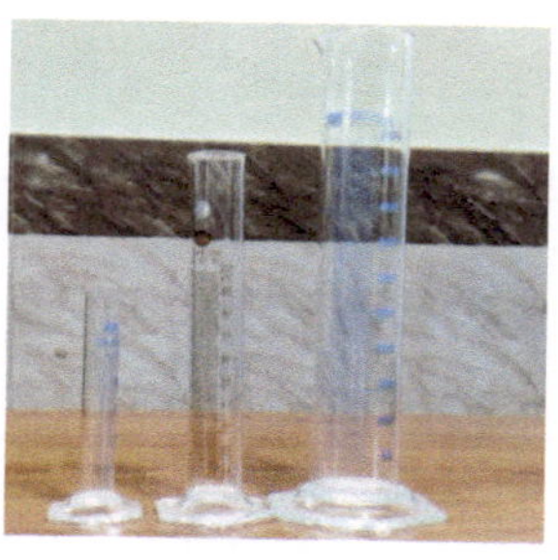

Measuring cylinder